RAIN NOISE

elle
heedles

rain
noise

℗℗

PARTUS PRESS

Oxford · Reykjavík

MMXXII

Rain Noise © Elle Heedles, 2022

First published in Great Britain in 2022
by Partus Press Ltd.
266 Banbury Road, Oxford OX2 7DL
www.partus.press

Book design and typesetting by
Studio Lamont.

Author portrait by Bogdan Zhvalevskyi.

A CIP catalogue record for this book
is available from the British Library.
ISBN 9781913196073

FSC
www.fsc.org
MIX
Paper from
responsible sources
FSC® C139361

CONTENTS

I will turn
in my name,
will you?

OUZELUM

This is the bird I bury
in your supersonic grave.
I ripped it from the evening sky
and bribed it with a riddle,
your name as the clue.
It held out its onliest wing,
made circles of the air,
flew backwards to meet me—
so ridiculous and rare
to see a ghost draw
hearts around a ghost.

RAIN NOISE

in the courtyard. There is rain
and there are stars. The rain collapses

through the tannins. I follow the reflection
of rain in the window of tenderness,

chase it through the trees to find someone
with your particular eyelashes. I will keep everything

someone could want: the cold, shade,
the vamp that plays on the hour, this unbelievable letter.

When the swings scrape in the wrong key, it is time to go home.
I tear a name from the middle part where the ducks swim.

I have mistaken you for sky, for waterfalls, but never
for an animal of stars. That is me. Echoes

from every corner. The dog
looks at me sideways. What did he make

of us that night, when I was a silver tooth,
a touch in time, and you the view

from the window, the grass under the needles.
All day the dog waits for a hymn from the pines.

The rain carries wishes
from the sky down.

PROPHET

Bought an orange notebook
to keep track of orange ideas.

Asked about the other colours,
where to keep the whales
and the moss,
myself.

Said orange is the colour of forgiveness.

Said what do you do.

Said milk apricots, photograph pests
for the almanac, lay inside the soil.

Said talk to the farmer
who stands at the edge of the field
burning a week's worth of garbage

into nothing, sending the nothing
of news and grocery lists
to the hens.

Said the last thing the hens see
is this orange woman
standing bare against the sun
as it sinks in.

LAST SUMMER

Forget the shade, the cold breeze
coming from there,
that way. A train

pulls into the warmth,
everyone's first love at once
in one foreign tongue.

The men lie in the grass
with their scripts
and loose clothes.

The trees keep the light
from their eyes, reading
their lines as men.

The man of the villa
catches a fish,
and I have nothing.

I have never read anything.
I hold onto the railing
upon leaving the train,

and a handful of candied lemons
in my dress pocket
pull themselves together.

RESPITE

Sitting on the porch of your heart,
the gentle heat pushes in.

There is wind, but it is above you.
It is urgent, and must act

quickly. If you can rise
to check the peach trees

over there, don't—
they are still only flowers.

The cat comes by with a corpse
to remind you of your unknown.

It's easy to leave the corpse
for the porch swing. There is no mess,

only back and forth and back and at some point
your eyes close, and the wind picks up.

BOO

The haunted moon is coming
into her own, a wrinkled sun
with more time to herself

than a ghost. Waning
is one eye closed one eye
open, each snicker
a stitch in the past.

How inviting,
this panic picnic—
the moon cannot keep
from constant surprise—

it is a thrill to be painted
over so many times.

DOG

A dog with half an ear
heads for the rock pools.

We have to share
what we have with others

to appreciate what we have
with others. I am bitten
on my right ear lobe.

The new tooth had barely arrived.
My ear scabs over, a warm

milk-film, a tongue held back
like a sharp tone in a cloud-bay.

Someone loved my ear so much
they claimed it. Now it's half-gone,

and I agree it's for the best—
half for all we've been through,
half for what will come.

Can you hear it?
The rain falls sharp on the ear
like a tooth.

PAINTER

brie melting on the sesame cracker,
brie melting under the grapefruit jam.
better to paint brie leaking
on a new canvas every day.
better than painting the brie
on itself over so much brie
that you could reach out and touch
its passionate ferment layers.
there is no room
for so much brie.
there is nothing
more like me than brie.

POPPY

Not enough people
to give flowers to, they die
quicker than a forecast.

I was taught if the lilac tree
grows too tall, too sentient,
it won't grow flowers.

Maybe next year I will be
the man to keep them,
bodies in a vase

that do not belong. The shreds
of petals will never reach
the dream that needs them

(piles of them, girl names,
one after the other).
How much are they?

I pull them from my dreams
and I am not a man, I am alive
in a tall order of unmistakable beauty.

MELANCHOLY

I am and the ocean
stands in. My waves
wash the shore clean.

A lost jellyfish serene
around my ankles.
The fishermen pass by—

none of their decisions are mine.

For a moment I thought
they would trade me all I've lost.
I send them somehow swimming
in water that was carried here,

not the other way around.
I will ignore the waves
when they decide to move.

CANAL

The kitchen is full of tenderness and dutch ovens.
I descend from the ladder with the blue one.

> The water is so blue, the bluest
> a green can be. You cannot see

> from your side of the river,
> but my nipples show through my shirt

> and they are magnificent. I look up
> the dream meanings of canals.

> Not floating in them, though
> I wish I could have done that.

> Floating beside.

> Just like the mirror game, our hands
> for walkie talkies. It is good,

> the connection. Sometimes a truck driver,
> but usually loud and bright. We exist

> like this for a while by the water
> like two thank-you bags in a zephyr.

There's a storm on the air.
I climb the ladder to put the vessels where they go.

WALK

Snow walk and bones
everywhere.

They take away the trees
when you're not looking.

Some still buried
crown to the sky,
roots warm and dry
in their boots.

Bones laying gently down,
faint. Good boy.

Still learning fetch.
No use.

What could you bring
back to me?

KITTY

Kitty lives with me. His body is long
as long as his name as long as his name
matters. When he thinks about me

he clasps his paws together. Forever
men have wanted to be loved by cats,
to resist dying, but they cannot.

Kitty has always been dead to me—
his gray hair, the whispers in his ears,
and the teeth where memory is held.

He is never angry, he only sharpens
his claws against my back a back
like so many others, turning away.

ROCK TUMBLER

the perfect gift for a mother
who is a rock collector.
when I go to the rock pool
I relinquish my purple
one rock at a time
my mother at the table
one rock at a time
each child creaseless and clean—
there is nothing so even
as a rock born again.
I surrender the birthstone
I stole from another pool—
better to keep hidden
the inner beauty of stones.
better to fade into oneself
one rock at a time.
I remind mother
that purple was a rare colour
once. we pass our purples
down until they are empty.
I love the smell
the dying stones make,
one at a time.

BIRDBATH

Now that I am far away
I see the grey rings around
the limitless order of words.

What will become of our summer
bodies? Which of us will be the last
to arrive at the baths? Migration

is only blood. Was it you
who told me about
an upside-down bucket

being something like a bell?
What rushes to the head?
Am I late, or is it the rain,

that airborne hope.

SOFT

Nothing in this house
is not taxidermy.

Closed mouth howl
at a storm with a name—

I'm your stuffed dog,
you're kind.

Some whistles
are impossible to me.

Dog skull loves a fireplace,
the cushion moulded

to a small, obedient body
like an eraser cut in half,

sharp and eager
to please.

Will you tickle the hair,
between the pads,

rub them of the cold?
Isn't this chasing rabbits?

Will you carry me
around, around,

carrying snow
by the scruff?

RED TRIM

The hem of my tartan peacoat
mocks my insides.
I lose track of the crumbs
laid out by poets before me.

The moon ends where my legs begin,
gently pitted and ebullient. The fat
sustains me through the loneliest cold—
wherever did my sparrow wing go?

Scratch the gold from the frame—
see how it was once red, too.
I core my apples and curse my seeds,
scatter myself for the birds.

A fine trail of bloodlets—they taste
of red trim, my sore sweater yoke,
the red winter branches that recoil
like poinsettia petals.

The red avadavat is a sparrow-
sized bird found in open fields.
It breeds in the monsoon season.

A strawberry with white seeds.

Delicious bird—
count my body
in.

PEEL

It was when I still believed
citrus grew one at a time.
It explained the curious
and the lonely. It made sense

that I would peel the scab
with one hand and eat it
with the other. I mistook it
for pith. One minute

you're in the garden
to gather an orange
in the company of oranges.

NURSE HEART-BREAKER COSTUME
WITH STETHOSCOPE

I make an appointment with the nurse.
We both wish I were someone else.
What needed to die? My arm was on the needle
when she dropped the cap—the blood was already deafening
itself to public memory. I got up to catch it, before I spilled
all over the floor. No, Nurse said, not you.
I keep my wits about me as evidence. My back hurts
from looking ahead of me into empty space for so long.
I think, when will the moon be big enough to see
with both of my eyes open? I think about my favorite croissant,
and the chiaroscuro pussy painting in the waiting room.
A godform floats in the air beside my head—it burns
my tight little brain from so many days of horoscopes.
I start to see the end like the fallout of a bath bomb
when Nurse finally finds me, and I remember my reasons
for walking into the kitchen that one time, right before the ooze
became a forever locus for undoing. Not a day goes by
that I don't feel top-bunk lucky. Each night I pray
to the ghost of sleepless nights, the waiting room magazine stench.
I miss the wool, I miss the invisible socks
and the pain of existing outside of oneself.

HOW TO CATCH A FRUIT

to get rid of decomposing fruits

search for the death-fruit

it is the fruit with the least remorse

leave out the sour remains

lick the blood from the spoon

go after the fruits

bare-hand the fruits open

so you can close in on the fruits

quickly so they cannot encourage others

kill the fruits you once looked up to

when it is warm and unbearable

so you begin to see

your life better without them.

COLD COUNTRY

I thought about you again.
The snow was here.
Everyone said it was too late.
You didn't say a thing.
Now it's bright.
The snow went somewhere else.
The people are at ease.
I count the stains on my window.
No, I count the ways the snow fell.
Until I lose the thread.
Then I pull the other end.
I think I know where this goes.
And the snow returns to me.
Pink and apologetic.
It is how it is.
With the lights on.
I listen for a footstep.
It's almost day.

ALISTAIR

Alistair can't go anywhere
without seeing berries.

Berry because the flesh holds
until pierced, then falls away.

The lingerie

will pay for itself, eventually.
Alistair eats a tomato like a fruit,

a one-handed bloody fist.
Eats through the centre fruit

like a girl. Sexy strands knitted

like hair into a sweater.
Try not to stare

when Ali is alone,
carrying fruit between rooms

in the golden hour.

TIDINGS

The bee in my room and I
we are reaching conclusions.
She is my best foot, I am
worthy of progress, a mink
ugly enough for a coat. She drinks
to all of it, a forever-toast.
What have we done,
my forgetful therapist,
to merit a front garden
and so many poets in our area?
They stop to wish us luck
and smell our beautiful dying
chrysanthemums, out of season.
Out of time, out of tune.
How happy can you be
to be here, one all-bright room
of so many too-bright places?
The poets can do nothing but hide
the keys and drink their tea.
The whole leaves and flowers
are a product of their environment.
They look nice floating
in a fortune, unable to leave.

BIRDHOUSE

My sieve is turning orange
because my oranges refuse.

I think about skin
stretched between so many

tangible hearts. I am a bird
because I save the seeds to scatter them.

Sometimes I forget one in my pocket.
I am a bird because I have a birdhouse

to rinse my seeds
and sing to them.

I sing about the girls
staring down the morning;

girls with flower names.
'Pretty flowers don't grow back.'

They do everything together.
I envy them.

CRÈME POUR LE VISAGE

I opened the foundation
looking for a reason
to buy it—my aunt's house
comes back to me, a neighbour

girl, sticky with almonds,
dizzy about the mailbox
and the wet blades
before noon. I steal it,

run from the store so fast
the field opens for me.

CRÈME POUR LES YEUX

Can you still see the night, back
when it was winter on the balcony
and we were the only animals
that were not stars, not warm

from a summer lightyears away?
You had yet to turn your eyes, so soft
I could not tell you anything—
not about the cold, the letters

I write behind my back, nothing—
and we pretended it was raining.

MANICURE

The day opens, a hand.
My nails are green, this time.
The river is warm
in some places, cold

from the waist down.
Wouldn't it be funny if—
that's not my hand.
But it's not up to me.

It is so democratic here,
washing my hands,
holding them underwater.
Look! They're in love!

While looking for the waterfall
someone clutches their hands
to my chest. Rain water
from the mountains.

Does that make me—

EWE

I call in my ewes
through hill and rune,
lost in the northwind switch grass,
moving the rainbow around.

Sheeeeeeeeeeepees!
Heeeeeeere, sheeeeeep!

A vagrant deer passes by,
the past from antlers hanging
pink pelt, pink pelt.

The little fellas will get used to me
and come running when they see me
rattling the grain bucket.

I call to my ewes—
yes, I hear all twelve.
I call to my dog.

I call in my ewes
to cancel the fever dream.

We congregate in the barn
like oats soaking overnight,
a bowl we prepare in the dark
to give the winter light a head start.

MOTORCADE

At the motorcade
stale and contemplative exhaust
fills all of my voids but one.

Why would anyone want to be
anything other than prey? In my arsenal:
broken crayons, a spool of paraffin,

goldfish pond enthusiasts, a pint
jug of milk, my bashful horse
always third out of the gate.

I shall call it Nibelung, after the stageplay
where you are the erudite apple farmer
and I am somebody's grandson.

We touch the statue's nose for luck.
The frosty horse butt and I are present
at the slow walk. So slow the peloton

heaves around us no problem. Nobody
rings their bell at us, not a single rooster
out of place. Every day we walk

between an aubade and a nocturne,
to know a country by its ghosts. We watch statues
fall—they bounce. We reach the boiling point

of milk. At the motorcade a stray bullet, licking
all of my friends. I run from you and you
pretend your gun is not smoking.

MIDNIGHT DOG

The chestnut halves
are hurting on the floor

without their hearts.
Someone has already been here

under the lamp-trees
two blocks from home.

The fall is fighting
for warmth. Someone's car

pulls out from over
your crushed autumn legs.

Someday better without them.

MAP

Tomorrow is supposed to storm
and already the subways

sound different, impossible
to move without feeling sorry

for the holes that will be
filled by the rain.

Goodbye, mice! Goodbye, ghosts!
Every six minutes until midnight
someone I know closes a window.

You feel how cool it is,
the rumbling in the darkness.

Maybe the trains are still running,
or maybe that's you, the tracks
closed like before you were born.

DEAD DROP

I remember the way home,
kick the ground into place.
Three rats on my way,
smaller than I remember.

Some forms we can never take.
Each brother-heart beats,
modest breaths marry mine.
When I step inside
my dutiful dark I am a half-
person, breathing fog indoors.

*

Tote Zauberratte,
starr mich nicht so an!
Hier gibt's nichts zu sehen.

*

No one will touch my dead rat.
I remove the heart and paper guts,
slip a note under the wounded skin.

'When Rie played the piano,
it was impossible to tell
how old she was.'

Suture soft and sweet. I hide
my rat in the open for you, hope
that you will see it on your way
and put it in your pocket.

That you remember me,
Death, though I have changed so much.

RAIN NOISE

You're getting up there,
and the sun is getting easier
on the eye. Remember the rain,
when it was all that mattered
to you outside of cutting bread thinly
so there would always be enough?
How quickly the sunset arrives
when you look at it through closed eyes.
What separates you from the raindrops
and the tulips on your head?
There is still rain where you are
when you loose yourself
from your small latchkey life.
People will talk about you like you
used to talk to the rain, beckoning
droplets of your own stench
so your bed might anchor, finally,
and sleep will sift up
through the floorboards, down
from the ceiling fan, and out
of your mouth. Talk to me,
tell me about a face,
how it could be anybody's but isn't.

RUTH

Bowled over with tears
a nation of women sing
through their personal keyholes
my sister's middle name.

Crowds arrived like rain
at the tail end of faith,
a flood of brackish water.

The draft under the morning door
announces the shadow I belong to,
now—who will run the shore
to blow cold air between my rings?

Who will remember the woman
with serene hair so serene
you could be a middle name.

BRACE

Like coins at the Laundromat
the braces don't quite fit
without a superstitious jiggle.
Maybe my crush will lose a tooth.

At the Laundromat like love
I rub the coins and lean
all the way into the mouth.
I hope I am not hurting

when I slip the pill into place.
My crush can brush their teeth
twice a day
but they will still be crooked.

My elbow on the metal bench
beside a magazine and fruit snacks
I watch my pining whites,
wait for the mouth to remember.

HAMLET

Everywhere the runners
practice good form.

I take a walk at night
before the runners
return to their ashtrays,

so I may see so many lights
around everything I know for certain.
Nobody is kissing.

Nobody steals a loganberry
between their lips to remember
the taste of the water fountain,
the stainless mouth.

Nobody stops the runners:
not milk, not moonbeams.

I am not ashamed.
I drink the entire fountain
empty.

What have I become?

IMPOSTOR

Dishonest fruit,
no ochre no crimson.
See when you lift the flap of skin,
the way you stare at nothing

and lose minutes off your life,
all that flesh? Nothing but green,
no fire, and you can hold yourself
in your own hands and rub yourself down

to know that you are alive.
Plums to outlive you.

CAKE

A lady with a gold necklace
calls me about the pear trees,
ready and waiting like a dark street.
In this day quietly humming
I hear the oven door open.
But who has followed me here
to this particular grove?
I say do not worry in case
it is my mother calling
to remind me none of this is mine
not even the eaten fruit.
And she is right to worry
because it is never okay to lie,
especially not about forgetting.

I return to my private Transylvania
when suddenly my room gleams
golden green like the desert
where we come from.
With the candles on the frosting
I hear the screaming children
I love and celebrate each day
without knowing where it comes from
or when it will arrive.

CRAFTS

Rain behind a wall
like needles dropping.
A headache is a neighbour
screaming my screams.

I live here too, this rain
is my rain. It is the same
as it has always been,
pools and gutters cascading

with good stuff. Someday
I will leave the poor door
and the craft lady, the marks
on her arms from gestural painting

and her master's voice,
the shawls she wore out
on her balcony, my balcony,
watching the development

from the nosebleeds.
I love my neighbours
like I love the rain,
rain behind a wall.

WASSERKOPF

would I rather be a dream
on the outside or on the inside?

now I lay
a mirror behind my head,

to see through closed lids
into half-empty jars.

I lie on a body of water
like a fish on a bed

of ice, the *Fischgräten*
where fish go to die.

Would I lie about
how I'm doing?

I clean myself of the mirror
with whatever water

I can find, a culprit
for these terrible dreams.

WALK

The vendor gives us cups without lids
and we skirt along the highway. It is the season
of walking without spilling hot orange
juice all over our hands.

There are too many lovers in town.
We duck under the moon, over the tracks.

No way to get to the trains where there is
nothing. A silent chimney holds its own,
spills night fog onto the empty bridge.
I can barely see you but I know you are there.

PENELOPE

I am not being cruel—
I knit the sweater in likeness
of myself. I need to know
if the colour of my heart
will betray me today.

In the garden, aliens
watch over me, petals
for lips and roots
that take. One sleeve
slightly larger than the other

like breasts, like plums.
Who is the wind in the sheets
to tell me I am not sincere?
I am above it.
Every face is two-faced,

asymmetrical and alone.
I hold the strands double—
no one is beside me
at the foot of trees, bending
to show restraint, gratitude.

TRAP

The stem still on the fruit,
a black, blue, raspberry
aftermath of a season
filled and overflowing.
The shimmer of a fish out of water—

verbatim. I am learning them.
I hang my berries
on a line. This is how I last
through winter
as hunger's pet.

It is a dying language
to lay the traps down
along the low river
masked by night-fruits
and kept secrets.

Hours go by—
much to do
about the little hearts
in the bushes,
my kill my kill.

The fish are blue-dead.
Like the berries,
lesser animals will arrive
to feed on them.
They will not be sad for long.

My hands are wet with it,
nails pearls in the dark.
Is it better to eat
the trap meat in one bite,
or save it, not knowing

when I'll eat again?
I double back
to the morning sun
my syntax clear
laid out before me.

I hear the traps close
gently gently
over a first step.

RAIN NOISE

It's not warm anymore,
not like yesterday.

I read about the storm
and all the sirens, listening

for the fish through the mirror,
a shared dream, the order of longing.

I am last in line.
The words wait

in lowercase.
I ask the rain to take

my place. I look outside,
just to make sure I am

alone, writing.

The keys under the mat
know where I'll be

in the dark. My room
fills with rain noise—

I am here. I am
alive, a pelagic fish

the water moves along.

Beneath each of us
memory hardens
into mud.

ENDLOVE

The twins
kiss each other goodnight

by pulling each other from the ground.
A bee always fails the one they love.

I wrote bee but meant flower.
Not pulling, but breathing.

The bee fades from the petal.
I misinterpret pain as song.

The boy or the bagged groceries,
the carcass or the bones.

The worm
or the half of itself it cuts away.

ACKNOWLEDGEMENTS

Sincerest thanks to the editors at *Oxford Poetry*, *wet grain*, and *Popshot*, who gave some of these poems their first home. My whole heart to Vala and Luke, Elisabeth and Zoë, Mina, Bogdan, Natalie, Jakob, Tyler, Christian, Anthea, Louis, Robin, Anna, and Daniel, for all of it. For my family, for my rats.